Albert Meltzer

ANARCHISM
Arguments
For and Against

NEW ANARCHIST LIBRARY

CONTENTS

INTRODUCTION

The Historical Background of Anarchism

It is not without interest that what might be called the anarchist approach goes back into antiquity; nor that there is an anarchism of sorts in the peasant movements that struggled against State oppression over the centuries. But the modern Anarchist Movement could not claim such precursors of revolt as its own more than the other modern working class theories. To trace the modern Anarchist movement we must look closer to our own times. While there existed libertarian and non-Statist and federalist groups, which we would now call anarchist, before the middle of the nineteenth century, it was only about then that they first became what we now call Anarchists.

In particular, we may cite three philosophical precursors of Anarchism: Godwin, Proudhon and Hegel. None of the three was in fact an Anarchist, though Proudhon first used the term in its modern sense (taking it from the French Revolution, when it was first used politically and not entirely pejoratively). None of them engaged in Anarchist activity or struggle, nor knew of such a thing as "Anarchism". One of the poorest though objective books on Anarchism, Eltzbacher's *Anarchism*, describes Anarchism as a sort of hydra-headed theory some of which comes from Godwin, or Proudhon, or Stirner, or Kropotkin, and so on. The book may be tossed aside as valueless except in its descriptions of what these particluar men thought. Proudhon did not write a programme for all time; nor did Kropotkin in his time write for a sect of Anarchists.

Godwin is the father of the Stateless Society Movement; which we may begin at once by saying diverged into three lines. One, that of the Anarchists (with which we will deal). Two, that of American Individualism, which included Thoreau and his school, sometimes thought of as anarchistic, but which equally gives rise to "Rugged Individualism" of the Goldwater school and to Tolstoyanism (so-called) and Ghandism. This second line of descent from Godwin is responsible for the "Pacifist Anarchist" approach or the "Individualist—Anarchist" approach that differs radically from revolutionary anarchism in the first line of descent. It is too readily conceded that "this is, after all, anarchism". Pacifist movements, and the Gandhian in particular, are usually totalitarian and impose authority (even if by moral means); the school of Benjamin Tucker — by virtue of thier "individualism" — accepted the need for police to break strikes so as to guarantee the employer's "freedom". All this school of so-called Individualists accept, at one time or another, the necessity of the police force, hence for government, and an *a priori* definition of anarchism is *no government*. The third school of descent from Godwin is simple liberalism.

Dealing here with the "first line of descent" from Godwin, his idea of Stateless Society was introduced into the working class movement by Ambrose Cuddon. A revolutionary "internationalist", and non-Statist socialism came along with the late days of English Chartism. It had some sympathy with the French Proudhonians. Those who in Paris accepted Proudhon's theory did not consider themselves Anarchists, but Republicans. They were for the most part master artisans, running one-man productive businesses. The whole of French economy was geared both to the peasantry and to the master artisan. Independent, individualistic, and receiving no benefit from the State save the dubious privilege of paying taxes and fighting, they were at that time concerned to find out an economic method of survival and to withstand encroaching capitalism.

These French and English movements came together in the First International. The International Workingmen's Association owed its existence to Marx, indirectly to Hegelian philosophy. But within the International, there was not only the "scientific socialism" of Marx, but also Utopian Socialism, Blanquism, English Trade Unionism, German authoritarian and opportunistic socialism, Republicanism, and the various "federalistic" trends. Bakunin was not the father of anarchism, nor the "Marx" of anarchism, as often thought. He was not an anarchist until late in life. He learned his federalism and socialism from the Swiss workers of the Jura, and gave expression to the ideas of the Godwinian and Proudhonian "federalists" or non-State socialists. In many countries, Spain and Italy in particular it was Bakunin's criticism of the ideas of Marx that gave the federalist movement its definition. (While to Anarchists, Marx is of course "the villain of the piece" in the International, it must be granted that without Marx, clearly defining one form of socialism there would have been no direct clash, no Bakunin clearly defining an opposite). There had grown up by 1869 a very noticeable trend within the International that was called "Bakuninist", but which was very clearly in one line of descent from Godwin and in another line from Proudhon. When the Paris Commune exploded in the face of the International, it was the parting of the ways (though this was deferred a little longer, and seemed to follow personal lines). From then on, Anarchists and Marxists knew by their different analyses and interpretations and actions during the Paris Commune, that they were separate.

For many years, all, the same, Anarchists continued to form part of the Socialist Movement. Marx had not succeeded in building a mass movement. The German socialist movement was more influenced by Lassalle; English socialism by the reformist and Christian traditions of Radical Nonconformity. Only after Marx's death, when Marxism was the official doctrine of German social-democracy, were Anarchists excluded from Socialist Internationals; Social-Democracy marched onto its own schism, that between English Liberalism masquerading as Labour on the one hand, and Social-Democracy on the other; and that between Majority Social Democracy (Bolshevism) and reformism. There were no more schisms in the anarchist movement; popular opinion made such figures as Tostoy into an anarchist (he was not; neither was he in the normal sense of the

word a Christian nor a Pacifist, as poularly supposed), but he
derived, if he were such, very clearly from the "second line" of
Godwinism. What we may perhaps call "mainstream Anarchism"
was singularly coherent and united, and it was given body by
the writings of a number of theoreticians, such as Peter Kropotkin.

After the bloody suppression of the Paris Commune, and
the repression in many parts of the world, Anarchism passed
into its well-known stage of individual terrorism; it fought back,
and survived, and gave birth to (or was carried forward in) the
revolutionary syndicalist movement which began in France. It
lost ground after the First World War, both because of the
growth of reformist socialism, and the rise of fascism; and
while it made a certain contribution to the Russian Revolution,
it was defeated by the Bolshevik counter-revolution. It was
seen in both a destructive and constructive role in the Spanish
Revolution of 1936.

By the time of the Second World War, Anarchism had been
tried and tested in many revolutionary situations and labour
struggles. Alternative forms had been tried and discarded. The
German Revolution had introduced the idea of Workers' Councils; the experience of the American IWW had shown the pos-
sibilities inherent in industrial unionism. Moreover, the "flint
against flint" in the arguement against Marxist Communism,
the lesson of what socialism without freedom meant in Russia,
and the failure of reformist socialism everywhere, helped to
shape the anarchist doctrine.

There were never theoreticians of Anarchism as such, though
it produced a number of theoreticians who discussed aspects
of the philosophy. Anarchism has remained a creed that has
been worked out in practice. Very often, a bourgeois writer
comes along and writes down what has already been worked
out in practice by workers and peasants; he is attributed by
bourgeois historeans as being a leader, and by successive bourgeois writers (citing the bourgeois historians) as being one more
case that proves the working class relies on the bourgeois leaders.

The idea of Anarchism survived the failure of anarchist organisation. The reconstituted I.W.M.A. ("the Berlin International") became in effect reformist; exiled organisations became fashionable but the idea unknown or ignored.

Republican France holds aloft the banner of the Social Revolution.

JUSTIFICATION OF ANARCHISM

That Mankind is Born Free

Our rights are inalienable. Each person born on the world is heir to all the preceding ages. The whole world is ours by right of birth alone. Duties, imposed as obligations or ideals, such as patriotism, duty to the state, worship of God, submission to higher classes or authorities, respect for inheirited privileges, are lies.

If Mankind is Born Free, Slavery is Murder

Nobody is fit to rule another. It is not alledged that Mankind is perfect, or that merely through his/her natural goodness he/she should not be submitted to rule. There are no supermen or privileged classes who are above "imperfect Mankind" and are capable or entitled to rule the rest of us. Submission to slavery means surrender of life.

As Slavery is Murder, so Property is Theft

The fact that Mankind cannot enter into his/her natural inheritance means that part of it has been taken from him or her; either by means of force (old, legalised conquest or robbery) or fraud (persuasion that the State or its servants or an inherited property owning class is entitled to privilege). All present systems of ownership mean that some are deprived of the fruits of their labour. It is true that, in a competitive society, only the possession of independent means enables one to be free of the economy (that is what Proudhon meant when, addressing himself to master artisan, he said, "property is liberty" which seems at first sight in contradiction with his dictum that it was theft). But the principle of ownerwhip, in that which concerns the community, is at the bottom of inequity.

If Property is Theft, Government is Tyranny

If we accept the principle of a socialised society, and abolishing hereditary privilege, and dominant classes, the State becomes unnecessary and unnecessary government becomes tyranny. "Liberty without socialism is exploitation; socialism without liberty is tyranny" (Bakunin).

If Government is Tyranny, Anarchy is Liberty

Those who use the word "anarchy" to mean disorder or misrule, are not incorrect. If they regard government as necessary, if they think we could not live without Whitehall directing our affairs, if they think politicians are essential to our well-being and that we could not behave socially without policemen, they are right in assuming that anarchy means the opposite to what government guarantees. But those who take the reverse opinion, and consider government to be tyranny, are right too in considering anarchy, no-government, to be liberty. If government is the maintenance of privilege and exploitation and inefficiency of distribution its tool then only anarchy is order.

THE CLASS STRUGGLE

Revolutionary anarchism is based upon the class struggle, though it is true that often even the best of anarchist spokesmen, striving to avoid Marxist phraseology, may express it differently. It does not take the mechanistic view of the class struggle taken by Marx and Engels. It does not take the view that only the industrial proletariat can achieve socialism, and that the victory of this class represents the final victory. On the contrary: had anarchism been victoriuos in any period before 1914, it would have been a triumph for the peasants and artisans, rather than the industrial proletariat amongst whom it was not widespread. Marxists accuse the artisans of being petit bourgeois which is a phrase used at the time by Marx; but there is a vast difference between the petit bourgeois of that day— cobblers, tailors, bookbinders, printers, goldsmiths, saddlers, etc., all productive workers engaged on their own account, and the non-productive "petit bourgeoisie" (Civil Servants, manufacturers, etc.) of today.

Any class may be revolutionary in its day and time; only a productive class may be libertarian in nature, because it does not need to exploit. The industrialisation of most Western countries has meant that the industrial proletariat has replaced the old "petit bourgeoisie"; and what is left of the "petit bourgeoisie" has become capitalist instead of working class, or the functionaries of the State.

As this happened, so the anarchist movement developed into anarcho-syndicalism, i.e. the idea that combinations of workers could, by organising themselves at their place of work and ultimately by running their own place of work, be the means of by-passing a State-run economy at the same time as eliminating a ruling class.

It has never been claimed (even, and especially, by Marx) that the working class were an idealised class (this belonged to the Christian Socialists, not the anti-idealistic Marxists or

Bakuninists). Nor was it ever suggested they alone could be revolutionary; or that they could not be reactionary. It would be trying the reader's patience too much to reiterate all the "working-class are not angels" statements in repudiation of working class struggle which purport to refute that the working class could not run their own places of work. Suffice it to say that only in heaven would it be necessary for angels to take over the functions of management.

"They're demanding time and a half for 5th level celestial Harmonies and the removal of Flight Time recorders."

ORGANISATION AND ANARCHISM

Those belonging to or coming from authoritarian parties find it hard to believe that it is possible to organise without "some form" of government. Therefore they conclude, and it is a popular argument against anarchism, that "anarchists do not believe in organisation". For instance:

They break up other people's organisations but are
unable to do anything because they do not believe
in building their own"

They may well break up organisations because they are dangerous, hierarchical or useless, but it is true to say they do not believe in building their own. It can well be admitted that particular people in particular places may have failed in such a task. It is true that in Great Britain, for instance, the anarchists have not yet succeeded in building up an effective organisation. This is a valid, internal criticism. But it is untrue to say that there *cannot be such a thing* as anarchist organisation. An organisation may be democratic or dictatorial; it may be authoritarian or libertarian; and there are many libertarian organisations, not necessarily anarchistic, which prove that all organisation need not be run from the top downwards.

It is significant that many trade unions, in order to keep their movement disciplined, and their members in an integral part of capitalist society, become (if they do not start as) authoritarian; but how many employers' organisations impose similar discipline? They cannot; because their members would walk out. They must come to free agreement, because the members have their independence ("property is liberty"!).

Only the most revolutionary unions of the world (I.W.W. of America, C.N.T. of Spain, etc.) learned how to keep the form of organisation of mass labour movements on an informal basis, with a minimun of central administration, and with every decision referred back to the workers on the job.

THE ROLE OF AN ANARCHIST IN AN AUTHORITIAN SOCIETY

The only place for a free man in a slave society was in prison, said Thoreau (after spending a night inside). It is a stirring affirmation, but not one to live by. The revolutionary must indeed be prepared for persecution and prosecution, but only the masochist would welcome it. It must always remain an individual action and decision as to how far one can be consistant in ones rebellion; it is not something that can be laid down. Anarchists have pioneered or participated in many forms of social rebellion and reconstruction: libertarian education, the formation of labour movements, collectivisation, individual direct action in its many forms and so on.

When advocating anarcho-syndicalist tactics, it is because social change for the *whole* of society can only come about through a change of the economy. Individual action may serve some liberatory purpose for the individual; for example one may retire to a country commune, surround oneself with like-minded people and ignore the world. One may then, indeed, live in a free economy. But one will not bring about social change. It is not because we think that "the industrial proletariat can do no wrong" that we advocate action by the industrial proletariat; it is simply because they have the effective means to destroy the old economy and build a new one, in our type of society at least. The Free Society (which we shall later describe)will come about through workers' councils taking over the place of work and by conscious destruction of the authoritarian institutions.

Workers Control

When advocating workers control for the places of work, we divide from those who merely want a share of management, or imagine there can be an encroachment upon managerial function by the workers. We want no authority supreme to that of the workers' council consisting of all the workers and not of their delegates. We reject 'nationalisation'—State control.

It should not be (but is, alas) necessary to explain that there are, of course, ways of personal liberation, and in some cases these may be necessary lest one starve, other than by mass action. But none of these can ultimately *change* society. The master artisan no longer plays an important part in production, as he did in Proudhon's day. One can get satisfaction by working on one's own; one may indeed have to do so by economic necessity; but the means of changing society rest with those who are working in the basic economy. The "gang system" of Coventry is sometimes advocated as a means of workers' control. But it is partial control only: power remains with the financial boss.

It can become a more pleasant method of working, within the capitalist system; but it cannot be a means of overthrowing the system. By all means let the system be alleviated; we do not oppose the reform of the conditions of work. But we do not pretend either that this has anything to do with building the free society.

The Anarchist as Rebel

It is not unknown for the individual Anarchist to fight on, alone, both putting forward his or her own principles and acting as a catalyst of rebellion. Examples come to mind of the M.P.T. Acharya, in India, and J.W. Fleming, in Australia, fighting on for their anarchist ideas, alone, the only one in the country. But it was not of their choice. Mostky, anarchists tend to form groups based on the locality in which they live. They may participate in other struggles (anti-militarism, anti-imperialism, etc.) or soley within the context of the class struggle (as "agitators" at work) or they may form organisations.

It is no part of the case for anarchism to say that the profession of its ideas changes peoples' character; or that the movement invites itself to be judged on anyone who happened to be around at the time. Organisations may become reformist or authoritarian. People may become corrupted by money or power. All we do say is that ultimately such corruption leads them to drop the name "anarchist" as standing in their way. (If ever the term became "respectable", no doubt we would have to choose a fresh one, equally connotative of libertarian rebellion!).

In all organisations, personalities play a part, and it may be that in different countries different schisms may occur. Some will say that there are different types of Anarchism — syndicalism, communism, individualism, pacifism. This is not so. If one wishes to cause a schism, purely because of personal reasons or because one wishes to become more quietist or reformist, it is no doubt more convenient to pick a name as a "banner". But in reality there are not different forms of anarchism. Anarchist-Communism, in any definition (usually that of Kropotkin) means a method of socialisation without government. An alternative idea, Anarchist-Collectivism (favoured by the Spanish Anarchists) was found in practice to be no different. If one is going to have no rule from above, one cannot lay down a precise economic plan. Communism, in the sense used by the Anarchists, is society based on the commune, i.e. the locality. Collectivism, based upon the place of work, is a division of the commune. But few anarcho-communists would dispute that unless the commune were very small (based upon the village, not upon the town) it would have to be sub-divided into smaller units, collectives, in order that all might participate and not merely their elected representatives. Otherwise, it would become merely industrial democracy. Whilst communism is an aim, syndicalism is a method of struggle. It is the union of workers within the industrial system, attempting to transform it into a free communistic society.

Whilst in a largely peasant country, like Bulgaria the anarchist movement was "anarcho-communist" because its natural form of organisation was the village commune, it could not be said that the aim of the Bulgarian anarcho-communist movement was any different from that say of the Italian anarcho-syndicalist movement. It is true that just as communism is not *necessarily* anarchist (we do not speak of the Russian type of Statism, State communism, but of authoritarian communism in its genuine form), so syndicalism need not necessarily be revolutionary. Moreover, even revolutionary syndicalism (the idea that the workers can seize the places of work through factory organisations) need not be libertatian; it could go hand in hand with the idea of a political party exercising ultimate control.

Non-Violence

Is pacifism a trend within the anarchist movement? The pacifism of Gandhi etc., is essentially authoritarian. The cult of non-violence as such always implies an elite, the Satyagrahi, who keep everyone else in check either by force or by moral persuasion. The general history of the orthodox pacifist movements is that they always attempt to dilute the revolutionary movement; but may come down on the side of force either in an imperialist war or by condoning aggressive actions

by the governments it supports. However, it would be true to
say that many Anarchists do consider it compatible with their
Anarchism to be pacifists, in the sense that they advocate the
use of non-violent methods (though usually nowadays advocating this on the grounds of expediency or tactics rather
than principle). This type of pacifist-Anarchism might be considered a difference of policy rather than of ideas; it should
not be confused with the "Tolstoyan Anarchism" (neither
advocated by Tolstoy nor anarchistic) which elevates non-
violence as an idol in itself.

Immediate Aims of the Anarchist

A "reformist" is not someone who brings about reforms
(he usually does not); it is someone who can see no further
than amelioration of certain parts of the system. It is necessary to agitate for the abolition of certain laws.

Sometimes the law is more harmful than the thing it
legislates against and there is a danger that abolition of the
law, bad as it is, might imply approval of the act itself (e.g.
suicide). But this is a risk that the libertarian must take. No
laws are worth passing; even those which are socially beneficial
on the surface (e.g. against racial discrimination) are quite
likely to be used wrongly. The Race Relations Bill and the
Public Order Bill were pressed for by liberals, and were used
against them. The Anarchist seeks to change attitudes and
minds. When those are altered, laws become obsolete and
unnecessary. At a certain point, the lawyers will be unable
to operate them. At a later date, the politicans will recodify
their laws so as to be able to continue in business. The re-
fusal of juries to convict thieves accused of theft above a
certain amount, led to the ending of the death penalty for
theft. The Witchcraft Act remained on the books until a
mere 30 odd years ago, but the Public Prosecutor only dared
rely on a few of its clauses, for fear of public ridicule. The
Tories passed the Trade Disputes Act in vindictiveness after
the General Strike, but public opinion was so much against

it they never could use it and until a solid trade unionist became Minister of Labour, it was worthless. The "1381" Act was useful for squatters to trip up the council. The odd part is that this act was entirely mythical. The myth persuaded many people it was legal to 'squat' so they did — and the numbers influenced the law.

It is necessary to carry on a resistance to any form of tyranny. It has been shown, too, very clearly in recent years that it is often useful to provoke the allegedly democratic forces of government into a position where it shows its true face of violence and repression. When governments see their privileges threatened, they drop the pretence of benevolence which most politicans prefer.

Anarchists are able to bring about disorder, but cannot seize power. Hence they are unable to take advantage of the situation they create. . . and the bourgeoisie, regrouping its strength, turns to fascism." **A Marxist**

Anarchists can, of course, "seize power" quite as much as strict teetotallers can get blind drunk. Nothing prevents them doing so, but they would require another name afterwards. Anarchists in power would not necessarily be any better or worse than socialists or liberals; they might be as bad as communists or fascists; they would, we hope, be totally ineffective because unprepared, their task is not to "seize power" (and those who use this term show surely that they seek personal power for *themselves*) but to abolish the bases of power. For power to *all* means power to nobody in particular.

It is true that if one leaves the wild animal of State power partially wounded, it becomes a raging beast that will destroy or be destroyed. It is this logic that causes anarchists to form organisations to bring about revolutionary change. The nature of anarchism as an individualistic creed has often caused many to view the question of such organisation as one that might well be left to 'spontaneity'', "voluntary will", and so on. In other words, to say that there can be no organisation (save that of propaganda only) until the entire com-

munity forms its own organisations. But it is shown by
events that a unity of resistance is needed against repression;
that there must be united forms of action even if there are
diversified forms of propaganda; and that even when, for
instance, workers' councils are formed, there are divisions between them on political grounds. Each political faction has
its representatives — united outside on party lines which are
able to put forward a united front within such councils and
to dominate and ultimately subordinate them. There must
therefore be an organised movement of anarchists if they
are to be able to withstand the forces of authoritarianism.
Such an organisation might well be obliged to rely upon acts
of individual terrorism (such as used in China and Spain) to
defend itself.

Workers' Self-Defence

The Marxist Leninists in times of revolution prefer to rely
upon the formation of a Red Army — a classic misuse of
revolutionary terms. Under the control of one party, the
"Red" Army is the old army under a red flag. We can see
only too clearly how this can become a major instrument of
repression. (Poland, after the first world war; Hungary, etc.,
after the Second). The very formation of an Army, to super-
sede workers' militias, will destroy the Revolution (Spain 1936).
The newest romantic idea of a Red Army is the Guevarist
notion of a peasants' army — combining the spontaneity and
freedom of a Makhnovista and Zapatista/Magonista (anarchistic) peasant armies with the discipline of the Party intellectuals. It has appealed immensely to the intellectuals
but found less favour amongst the peasants; it finds even more
favour among intellectuals the fewer peasants there are!
Regis Debray derides the workers' "self-defence" notions
of anarcho-syndicalism. Briefly, these are that the workers
use arms in their won defence, against the enemy at hand:
it is the idea of the people at work, armed, during periods
of social transformation. The Israelites have taken over

"We will shoot you down like partridges"

(Leon Trotsky, in his ultimatum to the defenders of Kronstadt, March 1921)

the "self-defence" idea with major success — not as liber-
tarians but out of national efficiency; indeed, so far as
military action is concerned, they have shown that it can
sometimes wage aggressive war successfully, or defeat a
Red Army led invasion. For purely political reasons, Debray
declined to take this into account; although it is an example
more apposite to Western industrial countries than is the
Castro movement, for instance. That the Israeli Army is
nationalistic is beside the point. Its mode of organisation
within the nation state is largely voluntary. It follows
patterns laid down by General Orde Wingate who understood guerrilla tactics better that Che Guevara, for all the
fact that he was an imperial soldier. The lack of discipline
in the workers' militias does not necessarily imply inefficiency.

How Will a Revolution Come About?

We do not know. When a revolutionary situation presents itself — as it did with the occupation of the factories in France in 1968 (or 1936); as it did in Spain in 1936 with the fascist uprising; or with the breakdown of the Russian Armies in 1917; or in many other times and places; we are either ready for it, or we are not. Too often the workers are partially ready, and leave the "wounded wild animal" of capitalism or Statism fiercer than ever. It may be purely individual action that sets off the spark. But only if, at that period, there is a conscious movement towards the free society, that throws off the shackles of the past, will that situation become a Social Change.

BRINGING ABOUT THE NEW SOCIETY

What Constitutes an Authoritarian Society?

EXPLOITATION–MANIPULATION–SUPPRESSION. The organs of repression, which consist of many arms of "The Establishment", for example:

The Apparatus of Government—the legislature, the judicature, the monarchy, the Civil Service, the Armed Forces, the Police, etc.

The Apparatus of Persuasion—the Church , the Press, TV, Radio, etc.

The Apparatus of Exploitation—the monetary system, financial control, the Banks, the Stock Exchange, individual and collective and State employers.

Most political reformers have some part of the unfree system that they wish to abolish (Republicans would abolish the Monarchy; Secularists would abolish the Church; Socialists would, or used to wish to, abolish the apparatus of exploitation; Pacifists would abolish the Army). Anarchists are infact unique in wishing to abolish all. Nobody but the Anarchists wishes to abolish the police. The Police (or the police in ultimate practice, which includes the Armed Forces) are the cornerstone of the State. Without control of the police, debates at Westminister become as sterile of result as debates of the West Kensington Debating Society (and probably less interesting). With German money, supplied by Helphand Parvus, Lenin was able to return to Russia and to pay Lettish mercenaries to act as police . He was the only one who could do so and in this one fact Bolshevik success is constituted.

Can One Do Without the State?

It seems to be generally agreed that we can do without *some* organs of the State; can we do without them all, altogether?

One cannot do the work of another (if the Monarchy does not have an army, it cannot save you from foreign invasion; and

the police will not get you into heaven if you do not have a church!) Any common sense codification of conduct would be better than the farrago of laws we have at present, which occupy both the lawyers and the politicians, the one interpreting the apparent desires of the other.

It is true that the government does take over certain necessary social functions. The railways were not always run by the State; they belonged to capitalists, and could equally in a future society belong to the workers. Even the police at times fulfil some necessary functions: one goes to the police station to find lost dogs simply because it happens to be there. It does not follow we should never find lost dogs if there were no policemen, and that we need to be clubbed over the heads in times of social unrest so that old ladies need not lose their dogs.

There was an old superstition that if the Church excommunicated a country, it was under a terrible disaster. One could not be married, buried, leave property, do business in safety, be educated, be tended whilst sick, whilst the country was excommunicated. It was not an idle superstition: so long as people believed in the Church, if it banned the country from the communion of believers, the hospitals (run by the Churh) were closed; there could be no trust in business (the clerics administered oaths); no education (they ran the schools); children could indeed be begotten, but not christened and were therefore barred from the community of believers; and unmarried parents could not leave property to their illegitimate children. One did not need the phisical reality of Hell to make excommunication effective. We are wiser now. But our superstition has been transferred to belief in the State. If *we* were to reject government there would be no education (for the government controls the schools), no hospitals (ditto); nobody could carry on working because the government regulates the means of exploitation, and so on. The truth all the time has been that *not the Church and not the State but we the People* have worked for everything we've got; and if we have not done so, *they* have not provided for us. Even the privileged class has been maintained by *us* not *them*.

The Myth of Taxation

The State myth calls into creation a second-hand myth, the money myth. According to this legend, all the wealth of the country is to be found at Waterlow's printing works. As the notes roll off the presses, so our wealth is created; and if this ceased we should be impoverished! An alternative but dated version was that these notes had to correspond with a quantity of gold buried deep in a mysterious vault (but it has long since been found that the government "welshed" on that!).

A secondary myth is involved: that the rich help the poor (and not vice versa): that by means of *taxation* taken from the

rich, those who are poor are "subsidized". The widespread belief in subsidisation is so great that it defies reasoned attack.
Many worthy people believe that if Lady X did not spend her
money on her yacht, that money could be mysteriously trans-
formed into an X-ray apparatus for the local hospital. They
do not understand that yacht builders cannot produce X-ray
equipment. Others think that those on National Assistance
are being supported by those at work. Yet the margin of un-
employment is painfully needed by the State to make the system of exploitation work. It is as necessary as the armed forces. Still more people believe there is a relation between the
way their wages go up and down and the wages received by
other people. In fact, in a competitive society they get what
they are able to command.

The Abolition of the Wage and Monetary Systems

To abolish the system of financial control, it is necessary
first to understand it. We put it here in a simple fashion. The
Government, or the effective financial controller which may
in some cases be *over* the government (the banks), assess the
national wealth. A corresponding number of bank notes are
printed, coin is struck, credits are granted to financial houses.
According to the degree of efficiency or inefficiency of the
government (which is the stuff of day to day press political
sloganeering, but need not concern us), the assessment, or
budget, may be correct or incorrect. The Chancellor of the
Exchequer may be "generous" or "niggardly", but according
to his assessment, so is the national "cake" and so are our various "slices". Salaries and wages are determined by social con-
vention, tradition, Government patronage, economic competition, hereditary influence, trade union bargaining, individual
enterprise and wildcat strikes, changing of jobs, and by various other means. According to their effectiveness, so is the
"slice" of cake each receives. The cake is, of course, the same.

In time of war, under "fair rationing", such a system need

not apply. In the second world war, we had "fair rations",
under which everyone, no matter what their income, received
only so many coupons for meat, reckoned by weight. This was
because it had been decided that meat should be shared equally, irrespective of income. The coupons had no value in themselves. Today they are only souvenirs in Carnaby Street. Then,
they were highly important.

Many communal products are equally available to all, either
on payment of a fixed sum, or free. The highways are free; it
would probably make no economic difference if the under-
ground railway was also free, bearing in mind the cost of
ticket collecting. We pay water rates, but may draw as much
as we like (it is rationed in the Sahara and may be costly).

A FREE SOCIETY would vastly extend the range of
communal products that would be free. It might be that
some products were in short supply and would have to be
rationed by some means. It could be by "labour value"
tickets (an hour's work per ticket, as a means of exchange)
as suggested by the collectivists; it could be by ordinary "fair
rationing" in the case of many items, food included; it
might be that some means of exchange, similar to money but
not based upon the wages system which immediately brings
equality, might be used. We cannot lay down economic laws
for a future *free* society. The authoritarian economist can
do so ("so long as I, or my party, are in power, the Pound
Sterling will be worth 100 new pence"); the libertarian can
only make such statements as "if you have inequality, you
must have a privileged class and government" — not because
the must is his dictum, but because it is something that
follows logically (just as does the statement that *if* there are
100 new pence in the pound there will be four lots of 25 new
pence, whatever you might call them).

A free society is not exactly an anarchist society, and far
from being a perfect society (utopia) if the latter is possible.
It is a society free from repressive institutions. Only in such
a society can we build up anarchism. The UTOPIAN SOCIETY
is one on which we should aim our sights. That is the direction

in which we should be moving, and the criterion by which we justify our success and failure. No anarchist seriously expects that one Monday morning he will read that capitalism has been abolished and that the State will fall before Tuesday when the rent-collector is due. Nor does the anarchist accept the Marxist-Lenninist argument that there is needed a "transitory stage" in which the State and bureaucracy must be strengthened, beyond all previous extent, so that it may wither away when unnecessary (as if any bureaucrat would ever find he was unnecessary). Transition is the period through which we are moving: the State will be superseded as the places of work are occupied (and re-started under self-management) and as free organisms replace direction from above.

Even the fascist has his utopia, a militarised society divided into class and racial strata. While he may never achieve it, his actions are determined by his vision of what he wants. The same applies to all who are not entirely deluded (in that they want one thing as a future utopia but entirely different actions are undertaken meanwhile; they perhaps peace "but prepare for war"). Even if the anarchist does not succeed within his lifetime, he does, to the extent that he is successful, modify society, mitigate tyranny, reform some evils.

The Employers Do Not Give Work

Work is not something, that is *given* by the employer. He may have the legal right to distribute work, but only because a demand for it has been made. *The wealth of the country is due to the workers.* The immigrants help to contribute to it (it is the emigrants who do not, but nobody objects to them!) It may be that in some technological society of the future, run by the State, in a sort of boss utopia, the working class will be displaced as a productive force. But this has not yet come about. It may be that technology will reduce us, as a productive class, to mere turners of switches and openers of the scientists' car-doors; to secretaries and receptionists; to janitors and clerks. Insofar as that happens, we must smash

that society. Those who revolt against ALIENATION see the
signs already.

Objections to Anarchism

Whenever one attacks present day society, one senses
the fears and prejudices of the average audience, they know
that society is a jungle today. But do not like to admit it.
Once one speaks of anarchism they bring forward objections
which are, in fact, criticisms of present-day society, but
which they think of as objections to a free society of the
future.

They fear murder, rape, robbery, violent attack — if
there were no government to prevent it. And yet we all know
the government cannot prevent it. (Read the "News of the
World"!) It can only punish where it finds it out, while its
own methods of repressive action causes far more damage.
The "cure" is worse than the disease. "What would you do
without a police force?" — Society would never tolerate the
murderer at large, whether it had a police force or not. The
institutionalisation of a body to look after crime means not
only that it "looks after" (and nourishes) crime, but that the
rest of society feels itself absolved. A murder next door is
the State's business, not mine! Responsibility for one's
neighbour is reduced in an authoritarian society, which
wishes to be solely responsible for our behaviour.

"Who will do the dirty work?" — This is a question
society has to ask itself, not merely the anarchist society.
There are dirty jobs which are socially unacceptable and poorly
paid, and nobody wants to do them. People are therefore
forced to do them (by slavery); or there is competition and
the jobs become better paid (and therefore socially acceptable);
or there is conscription for such jobs; or (as in England today)
the capitalist introduces immigration, thus putting off the
problem for a generation or two, or the jobs don't get done
(the street gutters aren't swept any more and we get deluged
with water shooting out from cars driven by graduate psych-

ologists). Only a clairvoyant could tell what an anarchist society would do; it is plain to all of us what it could *not* do (use force, since it would lack the repressive machinery). The question implies a criticism of prosperity and freedom, which bring problems in their train.

"If the Anarchists do not seize power, and have super-seded other forms of socialism that *would*, they objectively make way for fascism." There is really only one answer to dictatorship, and that is by the personal removal of the dictator. Anyone will seize power if given the opportunity; but if the seat is hot enough they might try to desist. We do not want to see a privileged class, and cannot put forward any claim that we would make a better privileged degree of leader-ship than any other.

Leadership

This is often a vexed question: do anarchists believe in leader-ship or not? Obviously not, because the leadership principle leads to the elite party, and the elite party to government. Yet for all that there *is* such a thing as leadership. Some people in some circumstances, do naturally "give a lead". But this should not mean they are a class apart. Any revolution in a factory where the majority have no revolutionary exper-ience, will at times "give a lead". But no anarchist would form an INSTITUTIONALISED LEADERSHIP. Neither too should he wait for a lead, but give one.

Can Public Opinion Itself Be of an Authoritarian Nature?

Most Certainly. Even in a free society? Certainly. But this is not an argument against a free society. There might well be, in a society controlled economically by the producers, prejudice against some minorities, for instance. But there would be no means of codifying prejudice, no repressive machinery against non-conformists. Only within a free society can public opinion become superior to its prejudices. The majority is not automatically right. The manipulation of the idea of a majority is part of the government technique.

Unity

One last objection is made against Anarchism, usually by those about to "come over". Why disunity in the ranks of those who take up a similar position on many stands? Why cannot we be all one libertarian left? Why any division at all?

Insofar as we form councils of action — workers industrial councils — even social groups based upon radical activity — we can be united with others of the libertarian left, or indeed (in the case of workers' councils) with people of the reformist or reactionary points of view. The expression of our anarchist opinions does not make us hermits. We still mix within society with people of all opinions and none. Anarchist groups need to keep alive their individual identity, but only a party machine could keep us from "speaking to outsiders".

THE MARXIST-LENINIST CRITIQUE OF ANARCHISM

It is very difficult for Marxist-Leninists to make an objective criticism of Anarchism, as such, because by its nature it undermines all the suppositions basic to Marxism. If Marxism is held out to be indeed *the* basic working class philosophy, and the proletariat cannot owe its emancipation to anyone else but itself, it is hard to go back on it and say that the working class is not yet ready to dispense with authority placed over it. Marxism, therefore, normally tries to refrain from criticising anarchism as such — unless driven to doing so, when it exposes its own authoritarianism ("how can the workers run the railways, for instance, without direction — that is to say, without authority?") and concentrates its attack not on *anarchism,* but on *anarchists.*

Let us put a stop to this chatter about the democracy of toilers, about freedom, equality, fraternity, the rule of the people and other such matters.

It has — whether one agrees with it or not — a valid criticism of the anarchists in asking how one can (now) dispense with political action — or whether one *should* throw away so vital a weapon. But this criticism varies between the schools of Marxism, since some have used it to justify complete participation in the whole capitalist power structure; while others talk vaguely only of "using parliament as a platform". Lenin recognised the shortcomings of Marxism in this respect and insisted that the anarchist workers could not be criticised for rejecting so philistine a Marxism that it used political participation for its own sake and expected the capitalist state to let itself be voted out of existence peacefully. He therefore concentrated on another aspect, which Marx pioneered, viz. criticism of particular anarchists; and this has dominated all Leninist thinking ever since.

Because of the lack of any other criticism of the Anarchists, Leninists — especially trotskyists — to this day use the *personal criticism* method. But as Lenin selected only a few well known personalities who for a few years fell short of the ideals they preached, the latter-day Leninists have to hold that all anarchists are responsible for everyone who calls himself or herself an anarchist — or even (such as the Russian Social Revolutionaries) were only called such (if indeed so) by others. They, however, are responsible only for fully paid up members of their own party.

This wrinkle in Leninism has produced another criticism of anarchism (usually confined to trots and maoists); anarchists are responsible not only for all referred to as anarchists, but for all workers influenced by anarchist ideas. The C.N.T. is always quoted here, but significantly its whole history before and after the civil war is never mentioned; solely the period of participation in the government. For this, the anarchists must forever accept responsibility! But the trots may back the reformist union U.G.T. without accepting *any* period in its entire history. In all countries (if workers) they presumably join or (if students) accept, the reformist trade unions. That is allright. But a revolutionary trade union must forever be condemned for any one deviation. Moreover, if broken it must never be rebuilt; the reformist union must be rebuilt in preference. This is the logical consequence of all trot thinking on Spain or other countries where such unions exist, proving their *preference* for reformist unions negative character which lends itself to a leadership they may capture; as against a decentralised union which a leadership cannot capture).

Petty Bourgeois

Notwithstanding this preference for non-revolutionary unions, and condemnation of the anarchists for unions built from the bottom up, all Marxist-Leninists have a seemingly contradictory criticism of anarchists, namely "they are petty bourgeois".

This leads them into another difficulty: How can one reconcile the existenec of anarcho-syndicalist unions with "petty bourgeois" origins—and how does one get over the fact that most Marxist-Leninists of today are professional ladies and gentlemen studying for or belonging to the conservative professions? The answer is usually given that *because* anarchism is "petty bourgeois" those embracing it—"whatever their occupation or social origins" must also be "petty bourgeois"; because Marxism is working class, its adherents must be working class "at least subjectively". This is a sociological absurdity, as if "working class" meant an ideological viewpoint. It is also a built-in escape clause.

Yet Marx was not such a fool as his followers. "Petty bourgeois" in his day did not mean a solicitor, an accountant, a factory manager, sociologist or anything of that sort (they were "bourgeois"—the term *small* it was 'petit', not "petty that qualified the adjective—meant precisely that these were not the same as bourgeoisie). The small burgher was one who had less privileges, economically, than the wealthy—but had some privileges by virtue of his craft. Anarchism, said Marx, was the movement of the *artisan worker*—that is to say, the self-employed craftsman with some leisure to think and talk, not subject to factory hours and discipline, independently minded and difficult to threaten, not backward like the peasantry. In England, these people tended to become Radicals, perhaps because the State was less oppresive and less obviously unnecessary. In many countries, however, they were much more extreme in their radicalism and in the Swiss Jura, the clockmakers, anarchism prospered. It spred to Paris—and the Paris Commune was above all a rising of the artisans who had been reduced to penury by Napoleon III and his war. As the capitalist technique spread throughout the world, the artisans were ruined and driven into the factories. It is these individual craftsmen entering industrialisation who became anarchists, pointed out successive Marxists. They are not conditioned to factory discipline which produces good order unlike a proletariat prepared to accept a leadership and a party, and to work forever in the factory provided it comes under State control.

That this observation was true is seen by the crushing of the commune in Paris and in Spain and throughout the world, especially in places like Italy, in the Jewish pale of settlement in Russia, and so on. It should be the task of an anarchist union movement to seize the factories, but only in order to break down mass production and get back to craftsmanship. *This* is what Marx meant by a "petty bourgeois" outlook, and the term having changed its meaning totally, the Marxists misunderstand him totally.

Vanguards

The reluctance of Marxist-Leninists to accept *change* is, however, above all seen in the acceptance of Lenin's conception of the Party. (It is not that of Marx). Lenin saw that Russia was a huge mass of inertia, with a peasantry that would not budge but took all its suffering with an Asiatic patience. He looked to the "proletariat" to push it. But the "proletariat" was only a small part of the Russia of his day. Still he recognised it as the one class with an interest in progress—provided, he felt, it was led by shrewd, calculating, ruthless and highly educated people (who could only come from the upper classes in the Russia of the time). The party they created should become, as much as possible, the party of the proletariat in which that class could organise and seize power. It had then the right and the duty to wipe out all other parties.

The idiocy of applying this policy *today*—in a country like Britain—is incredible. One has only to *look* at the parties which offer themselves as the various parties of the proletariat (of which, incidentally, there could be only one). Compare them with the people around. The parties membership are *far behind* in political intelligence and understanding. They are largely composed of shallow, inexperienced, youthful enthusiasts who understand far less about class struggle than the average worker.

Having translated the Russian Revolution into a mythology which places great stress on the qualities possessed by its leadership, they then pretend to possess that leadership charisma. But as they don't have it there is a total divorce between the working class and the so-called New Left, which has, therefore, to cover itself up with long-winded phrases in the hope that this will pass for learning; in the wider "Movement" with definitions at second-hand from Marxist-Leninism they scratch around to find someone really as backward and dispossessed as the *moujik,* and fall back on the "Third World" mythology . . .

The one criticism applied by Marxist-Leninists of anarchism with any serious claim to be considered is, therefore, solely that of whether political action should be considered or not. This is a purely negative attitude by anarchists. Wherever anarchists have undertaken it, because of circumstances, it has ended in disaster and betrayal of the revolutionary movement much as when Marxists have undertaken it.

THE SOCIAL—DEMOCRATIC CRITIQUE OF ANARCHISM

The early socialists did not understand that there would be necessarily a difference between anarchism and socialism. Both were socialists, but whereas the latter hoped to achieve socialism by parliamentary means, the latter felt that revolutionary means were necessary. As a result many early anarchists and socialist groups (especially in Britain) were interchangeable in working class membership. Something might come from political action; something by industrial methods; the revolution had to be fought as soon as possible; the one therefore was complementary to the other though it was recognised that they might have to follow separate paths.

This, however, changed because the face of socialism changed. It dropped its libertarian ideas for Statism. "Socialism" gradually came to mean State control of everything and therefore, so far from being another face of anarchism, was its direct opposite. From saying originally that "the anarchists were too impatient", therefore, the parliamentary socialists turned to a criticism of the anarchists levelled at them by people who had no desire to change society at all, whether sooner or later. They picked up what is essentially the conservative criticism of anarchism: which is essentially that the State is the arbiter of all legality and the present economic order is the only established legal order. A stateless society — or even its advocacy — is thus regarded as criminal of itself! It is not as a law but to this day, a police constable in court — or a journalist — will, for this reason, refer to anarchism as if it were self-evidently criminal.

Most upholders of any parliamentary system deliberately confuse it with democracy — as an ideal system of equal representation — as if it already existed. Thus ultra-parliamentarism is "undemocratic" — as if a few hundred men and a few dozen women selected at random alone had the right of exercising control over the rest of the country.

Since the Russianisation of "Communism", turning it away from both parliamentarism and democracy, it has suited the social-democrat to speak of criticism from the revolutionary side as being necessarily from those wanting dictatorship The anarchists, who can hardly be accused of dictatorship — except by politically illiterate journalists who do not understand the differences between parties must therefore be "Criminal" and whole labour movements have been so stigmatised by the Second International. This has been picked up by the U.S. Government with its "criminal syndicalism" legislation which is similar to that in more openly fascist countries.

No more than the Marxist-Leninists, the Social-Democrats are unable to state that their real objection to anarchism is the fact that it is against power and privilege and so undermines their whole case. They bring up, if challenged, the objection that it is "impossible". If "impossible", what have they to fear from it? why — in countries like Spain and Portugal, where the only chance of resisting Communist tyranny is the Anarchist Movement — do Social-Democrats prefer to help the Communist Party? In Spain up to the appearance of a Socialist Party when it was politically profitable the British Labour Party helped the communist-led factions but do nothing for the anarchist resistance.

Dictatorship of the proletariat is "possible" — only too much so. When it comes it will sweep the socialists away. But if the anarchists resist, the socialists will at least survive to put forward their alternative. They fear only the consequences of that alternative being decisively rejected — for who would choose State Socialism out of the ashcan for nothing if they could have Stateless Socialism instead?

In the capitalist world, the social-democrat objects to revolutionary methods, the "impatience" and alleged "criminality" of the anarchists. But in the Communist world, social-democracy is by the same conservative token equally "criminal", indeed more so, since it presumably postulate connection with enemy powers. The charge of "impatience" can hardly be levelled since there is no way of effecting a change legally; and the whole idea of change of parliamentary methods is a farce. Social-democracy, in the face of Marxist Leninism, gives up the fight without hope. It has nothing to offer. There can be no change from Fascism to Social-Democracy because no constitutional methods offer tnemselves — but at least in that case, they could in the past rely on foreign support changing the system. Their interpretation of socialism apparently forbids them to take this view in regard to the Soviet Union and its satellites. They have no ideas on how to change. They hope that nationalists and religious dissidents will put through a bit of liberalism that will ease the pressure. Yet anarchism offers a revolutionary attack upon the communist countries that is not only rejected by the social democrats; in power, they unite with other capitalist powers to harass and suppress that attack.

THE LIBERAL-DEMOCRATIC OBJECTION TO ANARCHISM

Liberal-Democracy or non-fascist conservatism is afraid to make direct criticisms of anarchism because to do so undermines the whole reasoning of liberal democracy. It therefore resorts to falsification: anarchists are equated with Marxists (and thereby the whole Marxist criticism of anarchism ignored). The most frequent target of attack is to suggest that Anarchism is some form of Marxism plus violence, or some extreme form of Marxism.

The reason liberal democracy has no defence to offer against real anarchist argument is because liberal democracy is using it as its apologia in the defence of "freedom" yet circumscribing walls around it. It pretends that parliamentarism is some form of democracy, but though sometimes prepared to admit (under pressure) that parliamentarism is no form of democracy at all, occasionally seeks to find ways of further democratising it. The undoubtedly dictatorial process that a few people, once elected, by fair means or foul, have a right to make decisions for the majority, is covered up by a defence of the Constitutional Rights or even the individual liberty, of those members of Parliament . . . Burke's dictum that they are representatives, not delegates, is quoted ad nauseum (as if this reactionary politician had bound the British people for ever, though he, as he is self-admitted, did not seek to ask their opinions on the matter once).

Liberal economics are almost as dead as the Dodo. What rules is either the monopoly of the big firms, or of the State. Yet laisser faire economics remain embodied aspirations of the Tory Party which they never implement. They object to the intervention of the State in business. But they never care to carry the spirit of competition too far. There is no logical reason why there should be any restriction on the movement of currency and this is good Tory policy (though never implemented! Not until the crisis is over!) Why should we not be able to deal in gold pieces or U.S. dollars or Maria Theresa thalers or francs or Deutschmarks or even devalued Deutschmarks? The pound sterling would soon find its own level, and if it were devalued, so much the worse for it. But why stop there? If we can choose any currency we like free socialism could co-exist with capitalism and it would drive capitalism out.

State socialism can co-exist with capitalism as long as the State gives a place to the existence of capitalism (it drives it out in Russia, allows a small place in other Communist countries).

But once free socialism competes with capitalism — as it would if we could choose to ignore the State's symbolic money and deal in one of our own choosing which reflected real work values — who would choose to be exploited? Quite clearly no laisser-faire economist who had to combine his role with that of party politician (and therefore practical man) would allow things to go that far.

Liberal democracy picks up one of the normal arguments against anarchism which begin on the right wing; namely it begins with the objections against socialism — that is Statism — but if there is an anti-Statist socialism that is in fact more liberal than itself, then it is "criminal". If it is not, then it seeks law to make it so.

This argument is in fact beneath contempt, yet it is one which influences the press, police and judiciary to a surprising extent. But in fact anarchism as such (as distinct from specific anarchist organisations) could never be illegal, because no laws can make people love the State. It is only done by false ideals such as describing the State as a "country".

The fact is that liberal democracy seldom voices any arguments against anarchism as such — other than relying upon prejudice — because its objections are purely authoritarian, and unmask the innate Statism and authoritarianism of liberalism. Nowadays conservatives like to appropriate the name "liberalism" to describe themselves as if they were more receptive to freedom than socialists. But their libertarianism is confined to keeping the State out of interfering in their business affairs. Once anarchism makes it plain that it is possible to have both social justice and to dispense with the State they are shown in their true colours. Their arguments against State Socialism and Communism may sound "libertarian", but their arguments against Anarchism reveal that they are essentially authoritarian. That is why they prefer to rely upon inuendo, slanders and false reporting, which is part and parcel of the Establishment anti-anarchism, faithfully supported by the media.

THE FASCIST OBJECTION TO ANARCHISM

The fascist objection to anarchism is, curiously enough, more honest than that of the Marxist, the Liberal or the Social Democrat. Most of these will say—if pressed—that Anarchism is an ideal, perhaps imperfectly understood, but either impossible of achievement or possible only in the distant future. The Fascist, on the contrary, admits its possibility; what is denied is its desirability.

The right wing authoritarian (which term includes many beyond those naming themselves fascists) worships the very things which are anathema to Anarchists, especially the State. Though the conception of the State is idealised in fascist theory, it is not denied that one could do without it. But the "first duty of the citizen is to defend the State" and it is high treason to oppose it or advocate its abolition

Sometimes the state is disguised as the "corporate people" or "the nation" giving a mystic idea of the State beyond the mere bureaucratic apparatus of rule. The forces of militarism and oppression are idealised (after the German Emperor who said that universal peace was "only a dream—not even a good dream"). Running throughout right wing patriotism is a mystical feeling about the "country", but though Nazis in particular sometimes have recourse to an idealisation of the "people" (this has more of a racial than popular connotation in German) it is really the *actual soil* that is held sacred, thus taking the State myth to its logical conclusion. For the Anarchist this, of course, is nonsense. The nonsense can be seen in its starkest form with the followers of Franco who killed off so many Spaniards, hankering for the barren rock of Gibraltar; especially in General Millan de Astray who wanted to kill off "bad Spaniards" and erradicate Catalans and Basques in the name of unitary Spain (thus, as Unamuno pointed out, making Spain as "one-armed and one-eyed" as the notorious General was himself).

Anarchism is clearly seen by Fascists as a direct menace and not a purely philosophical one. It is not merely the direct of Anarchists but the thing itself which represents the evil (the media is just getting around to picking up these strands in fascist thinking, ironing them out nicely, and presenting them in the "news" stories). Hitler regarded the authoritarian state he had built as millenial (the thousand year state) but he new it could be dismembered and rejected. His constant theme was the danger of this and while he concentrated (for political reasons) attacks on a totalitarian rival, State Communism (since Russia presented a military menace), his attcks on "cosmopolitanism" have the reiterated theme of anti-anarchism.

"Cosmopolitanism" and "Statelessness" was one of the "crimes" with which he associated Jews (as indeed does the totalitarian communism of Russia), though plainly since his day large numbers of them have reverted to nationalism and a strong state. The theme of "Jewish domination" goes hand in hand with "anarchistic destruction of authority, morals and discipline", since for him personal freedom was bad in itself. (Only national freedom is permissable). Insofar as one can make sense of his speeches (which are sometimes deceptive since he follows different strands of thought according to the way he could sway an audience), he believes "plunging into anarchy" of a country (abolition of State restraints) willl lead to chaos, which will make it possible for a dictatorship other than one in the people's interests to succeed.

This Nazi propaganda is echoed by the media today; "plunging the country into anarchy would be followed by a Communist or extreme right-wing dictatorship" is taken from a current newspaper leader, and echoed almost daily.

Hitler did not confuse State Communism with anarchism (as Franco did deliberately, for propaganda purposes, to try to eradicate anarchism from history). He equates communism with "Jewish domination" and the case against the Jews (in original Nazi thinking) that they are a racially pure people who will gain world conquest over helots like the Germans

if a "Master Race" does not control the Germans and keep
the rival Sate out. In a condition of freedom the German
"helots" would revert to anarchy, just as the racially
"inferior" Celts of France threw out the Norman Nordic
overlords (the Houston Chamberlain version of the French
Revolution). Later, of course, when Nazism became a mass
party it was expedient to amend this to saying the *Germans*
were the Master Race, but this was not the original Nazi
philosophy nor was it privately accepted by the Nazi leaders
("the German people were not worthy of me.") But they
could hardly tell mass meetings that they were all "helots".
At least, not until their power was complete.

To sum up the fascist objection to Anarchism: it is not
denied the abolition of the State can come about, but if so,
given economic, social and political freedom, the "helots" —
who are "naturally inclined" to accept subjection from
superior races — will seek for masters. They will have a
nostalgia for "strong rule".

In Nazi thinking, strong rule can only come from racially
pure members of the "Master Race" (something a little more
than a class and less than a people), which can be constructive
masters (i. e. the "Aryans"), or a race which has had no con-
tact with the "soil" and will be thus destructive. (This iden-
tification of the Jews would have to be completely revised
in light of present day Israel).

In other types of Fascist thinking, given freedom, the
people will throw off all patriotic and nationalistic alle-
giances and so the "country" will cease to be great. This
is the basis of Mussolini's fascism, and of course, it is perfectly
true, bearing in mind that "the country" is his synonym for the
State and his only conception of greatness is militaristic. The
frankest of all is the Spanish type of fascism which sought to
impose class domination of the most brutal kind and made it
plain that its opposition to anarchism was simply in order to
keep the working class down; if necessary, the working class
may be decimated in order to crush anarchism.

It is true of all political philosophies and blatant with

the fascist one that its relationship to anarchism throws a clear light upon itself.